Pisces

SALLY KIRKMAN

Pisces

The Art of Living Well and Finding
Happiness According to Your Star Sign

HODDER

First published in Great Britain in 2018 by Hodder & Stoughton
An Hachette UK company

1

A CIP catalogue record for this title is available from the British Library

Hardback ISBN 978 1 473 67665 7

Typeset in Celeste 11.5/17 pt by Palimpsest Book Production Limited,
Falkirk, Stirlingshire

Printed in the United States of America by LSC Communications

Hodder & Stoughton policy is to use papers that are natural,
renewable and recyclable products and made from wood grown in
sustainable forests. The logging and manufacturing processes are expected
to conform to the environmental regulations of the country of origin.

Hodder & Stoughton Ltd
Carmelite House
50 Victoria Embankment
London EC4Y 0DZ

www.hodder.co.uk

Contents

• • • • •

Introduction

• • • • •

Before computers, books or a shared language, people were fascinated by the movement of the stars and planets. They created stories and myths around them. We know that the Babylonians were one of the first people to record the zodiac, a few hundred years BC.

In ancient times, people experienced a close connection to the earth and the celestial realm. The adage 'As above, so below', that the movement of the planets and stars mirrored life on earth and human affairs, made perfect sense. Essentially, we were all one, and ancient people sought symbolic meaning in everything around them.

We are living in a very different world now, in

which scientific truth is paramount; yet many people are still seeking meaning. In a world where you have an abundance of choice, dominated by the social media culture that allows complete visibility into other people's lives, it can be hard to feel you belong or find purpose or think that the choices you are making are the right ones.

It's this calling for something more, the sense that there's a more profound truth beyond the objective and scientific, that leads people to astrology and similar disciplines that embrace a universal truth, an intuitive knowingness. Today astrology has a lot in common with spirituality, meditation, the Law of Attraction, a desire to know the cosmic order of things.

Astrology means 'language of the stars' and people today are rediscovering the usefulness of ancient wisdom. The universe is always talking to you; there are signs if you listen and the more you tune in, the more you feel guided by life. This is one of astrology's significant benefits, helping you to make sense of an increasingly unpredictable world.

Used well, astrology can guide you in making the best possible decisions in your life. It's an essential skill in your personal toolbox that enables you to navigate the ups and downs of life consciously and efficiently.

About this book

Astrology is an ancient art that helps you find meaning in the world. The majority of people to this day know their star sign, and horoscopes are growing increasingly popular in the media and online.

The modern reader understands that star signs are a helpful reference point in life. They not only offer valuable self-insight and guidance, but are indispensable when it comes to understanding other people, and living and working together in harmony.

This new and innovative pocket guide updates the ancient tradition of astrology to make it relevant and topical for today. It distils the wisdom of the star signs into an up-to-date format that's easy to read and digest, and fun and informative too. Covering a broad range of topics, it offers you insight and understanding into many different areas of your life. There are some unique sections you won't find anywhere else.

The style of the guide is geared towards you being able to maximise your strengths, so you can live well and use your knowledge of your star sign to your advantage. The more in tune you are with your zodiac sign, the higher your potential to lead a happy and fulfilled life.

The guide starts with a quick introduction to your star sign, in bullet point format. This not only reveals your star sign's ancient ruling principles, but brings astrology up-to-date, with your star sign mission, an appropriate quote for your sign and how best to describe your star sign in a tweet.

The first chapter is called 'Be True To Your Sign' and is one of the most important sections in the guide. It's a comprehensive look at all aspects of your star sign, helping define what makes you special, and explaining how the rich symbolism of your zodiac sign can reveal more about your character. For example, being born at a specific time of year and in a particular season is significant in itself.

This chapter focuses in depth on the individual attributes of your star sign in a way that's positive and uplifting. It offers a holistic view of your sign and is meant to inspire you. Within this section, you find out the reasons why your star sign traits and characteristics are unique to you.

There's a separate chapter towards the end of the guide that takes this star sign information to a new level. It's called 'Your Cosmic Gifts and Talents' and tells you what's individual about you from your star sign perspective. Most importantly, it highlights your skills and strengths, offering you clear examples of how to make the most of your natural birthright.

The guide touches on another important aspect of your star sign, in the chapters entitled 'Your Shadow Side' and 'Your Star Sign Secrets'. This reveals the potential weaknesses inherent within your star sign, and the tricks and habits you can fall into if you're not aware of them. The star sign secrets might surprise you.

There's guidance here about what you can focus on to minimise the shadow side of your star sign, and this is linked in particular to your opposite sign of the zodiac. You learn how opposing forces complement each other when you hold both ends of the spectrum, enabling them to work together.

Essentially, the art of astrology is about how to find balance in your life, to gain a sense of universal or cosmic order, so you feel in flow rather than pulled in different directions.

Other chapters in the guide provide revealing information about your love life and sex life. There are cosmic tips on how to work to your star sign strengths so you can attract and keep a fulfilling relationship, and lead a joyful sex life. There's also a guide to your love compatibility with all twelve star signs.

Career, money and prosperity is another essential section in the guide. These chapters offer you vital information on your purpose in life, and how to make the most of your potential out in the world. Your star sign skills and strengths are revealed, including what sort of job or profession suits you.

There are also helpful suggestions about what to avoid and what's not a good choice for you. There's a list of traditional careers associated with your star sign, to give you ideas about where you can excel in life if you require guidance on your future direction.

Also, there are chapters in the book on practical matters, like your health and well-being, your food and diet. These recommend the right kind of exercise for you, and how you can increase your vitality and nurture your mind, body and soul, depending on your star sign. There are individual yoga poses and tarot cards that have been carefully selected for you.

Further chapters reveal unique star sign information about your image and style. This includes whether there's a particular fashion that suits you, and how you can accentuate your look and make the most of your body.

There are even chapters that can help you decide where to go on holiday and who with, and how to decorate your home. There are some fun sections, including ideal gifts for your star sign, and ideas for films, books and music specific to your star sign.

Also, the guide has a comprehensive birthday section so you can find out which famous people share your birthday. You can discover who else is born under your star sign, people who may be your role models and whose careers or gifts you can aspire to. There are celebrity examples throughout the guide too, revealing more about the unique characteristics of your star sign.

At the end of the guide, there's a Question and Answer section, which explains the astrological terms used in the guide. It also offers answers to some general questions that often arise around astrology.

This theme is continued in a useful section entitled Additional Information. This describes the symmetry of astrology and shows you how different patterns connect the twelve star signs. If you're a beginner to astrology, this is your next stage, learning about the elements, the modes and the houses.

View this book as your blueprint, your guide to you and your future destiny. Enjoy discovering astrological revelations about you, and use this pocket guide to learn how to live well and find happiness according to your star sign.

A QUICK GUIDE TO PISCES

• • • • •

Pisces Birthdays: 19 February to 20 March

Zodiac Symbol: The Fishes

Ruling Planet: Jupiter – traditional; Neptune – modern

Mode/Element: Mutable Water

Colour: Sea-green, aquamarine, colours of the sea

Part of the Body: Feet

Day of the Week: Thursday

Top Traits: Romantic, Compassionate, Creative

Your Star Sign Mission: to offer caring

and kindness where it's needed most, to believe in miracles

Best At: poetic sensibilities, empathy, self-sacrifice and redemption, sensitivity and vulnerability, going with the flow, living on or close to water, daydreaming, craving gorgeous shoes

Weaknesses: addictive tendencies, deceitful, gullible, lacks boundaries, lost soul

Key Phrase: I dream

Pisces Quote: 'Imagination is more important than knowledge.' Albert Einstein

How to describe Pisces in a Tweet: A seeker – ethereal & empathic. Wafts through life in a haze of romantic dreams & spiritual yearnings. Saviour of lost souls & small animals

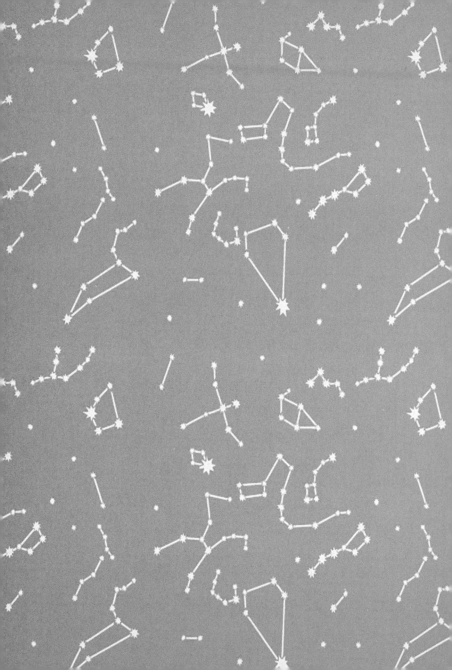

Be True To Your Sign

• • • • •

Pisces is the last sign of the zodiac and is said to contain a little of all the other eleven signs within it. On the one hand, this bestows upon you infinite wisdom and knowledge and, on the other hand, it conjures up the symbol of Pisces being the cosmic dustbin. This is where everything ends up, but also where it begins.

At one level, Pisces' role is to let go of what's no longer needed and prepare the way for the beginning of a new zodiac cycle. Pisces' season leads up to the Sun's entry into the first sign of the zodiac, Aries, on the day of the Equinox, heralding spring in the northern hemisphere.

During Pisces' birthday season, there are already

glimmers of life returning as winter begins to fade and the warmth slowly returns to the earth. Like all of the mutable signs, Pisces represents a change in season, as you discard the old to make way for the new.

It's not surprising you have a boundless nature that wants to experience life, the universe and everything, as Pisces' co-rulers are Jupiter and Neptune, two of the big planets. In mythology, Jupiter was a sky god, and Neptune was god of the sea. Both entities are vast and endless, whether you're soaring through the sky out into the cosmos, or diving down into the dark depths of the ocean.

The season of Lent takes place during your birthday month, with its themes of penance and prayer, reflection and preparation. Traditionally, this is a time of sacrifice and withdrawal, when you consider what you're willing to give up, atone for your sins and practise self-denial.

Some Pisces individuals take these themes to heart completely. You can choose to devote your life to prayer or withdraw from conventional society to lead a sacred or spiritual path. The Age of Pisces coincided with the rise of Christianity, and the fish, your zodiac symbol, was a religious symbol.

Pisces' zodiac symbol depicts two fishes swimming in opposite directions, joined by a cord. This alludes to your searching, changeable nature, which goes off in different directions, seeking answers to a myriad of questions. You have one foot in reality, but another part of you wants to go beyond what's possible, to explore alternative dimensions, to seek out all that's magical and inexplicable in life.

As a Pisces, you are the romantic of the zodiac, in every sense of the word. You believe in all aspects of love and your archetypal nature is kind and compassionate, sensitive and forgiving. Your artistic spirit seeks inspiration in the world, and your quest in life goes beyond the personal, to see what lies past an ordinary existence and the confines of the ego.

You are often described as being otherworldly or ethereal, and it's true that you have a delicate nature. You wear your heart on your sleeve, and you are typically vulnerable and impressionable. Add to this the fact that you're one of the emotional water signs, and you respond to life through your feelings.

You feel deeply, you can be easily wounded by insensitivity and you pick up on other people's feelings. Your sensitive nature is finely attuned to emotion, noise, colour, even vibration. This means you often have psychic abilities and, most significantly, your empathy knows no bounds.

You feel joy and sadness, happiness and sorrow more intensely than other people. This can be a blessing but also a weakness, if you don't learn to filter out what's harmful or what's not yours to deal with.

Your traditional ruling planet is Jupiter, the planet linked to expansion, and sometimes you have to rein in your big-hearted and all-giving personality, especially when you give so much that you have nothing left for yourself. Learning to love and nurture yourself is a crucial Pisces lesson.

Your modern planet, Neptune, was discovered in 1846, and the events and significant developments at the time a planet was found can reveal a lot about the planet's symbolism.

Neptune was discovered during an era of significant developments in photography and film, pharmaceuticals, cults and the occult, the spiritual movement and the Romantics. Neptune, therefore, is considered the planet of the imagination, mysticism, illusion and fantasy. As a Pisces, it helps if you can find an outlet for your vivid imagination and a vessel for your dreams and your love of make-believe.

The world of escapism is Neptune's domain and includes poetry, music and art, romantic love and spiritual love, wine and song. It's sometimes said of your sign that you are either a saint or a sinner, and both are ways to escape reality. A preferred strategy perhaps is to take a little bit of each and entwine them into the different strands of your intricate personality.

Complexity is part of the Pisces psyche, fitting your role as the last sign of the zodiac. The wheel of astrology has come full circle, gathering insight, knowledge and understanding along the way. It culminates with your sign, signifying the universal as well as the personal, the collective as well as the individual. One of your life lessons is to find where you belong, not only alongside other people but in the wider cosmos too.

In astrology, Pisces rules the twelfth house, with its themes of 'hidden' things: solitude, spirituality and mysticism. This sector of the horoscope is also called 'the house of self-undoing'. This means perhaps that being a Pisces is to learn how to lose yourself so you can find yourself, to take off the mask you wear so you can become who you really are. Alternatively, it suggests breaking free of the ego in the search for oneness and unity.

You are the zodiac's daydreamer and visionary, whose explorations push back the boundaries of existence as far as they will go. You go beyond what's normal to seek out what's extraordinary, to find where awe and wonder reside. The powers of belief, hope and love accompany you on your journey.

Your Shadow Side

Pisces' shadow side is easy to imagine if you consider the 'saint and sinner' theme inherent within your archetype, and the fact that your zodiac symbol is two fishes swimming in opposite directions. It can be said that one fish is chasing after nirvana, while the other fish is swimming down into the void.

In other words, you can 'ascend to heaven' via a route that's creative or spiritual, artistic or mystical, or you can 'descend to hell' and spiral down into a life of addiction. The trick is to become dependent on activities and values that lift you up and bring salvation, not annihilation. One way to escape addiction is through connection and, for you as a Pisces, this extends to love in all its forms: self-love, romantic love and divine love.

It also helps to find a waterproof vessel for the deep well of your emotions. Pisces' twelfth house has another name, the 'vale of tears', and you're a water sign. This is an excessive amount of watery emotion, and you can dissolve into tears at the drop of a hat.

Sometimes you have a reputation for being a 'crybaby'; your strong emotions can flood your being. This is when you need to learn to surf the waves of life and know that there will be times of joy as well as sorrow. Just as the sea's tides ebb and flow, your moods too will change and shift, and rarely remain constant.

As a Pisces, it is essential to stay in touch with reality and have a sound anchor in your life. Without structure or boundaries that contain you and protect you, you can lose your way, give in to confusion or go round in circles with no clear path in sight.

At its most extreme, this can turn into delusional behaviour or lead you down a path that's crazy and unruly. You become so out of touch with reality that you're away with the fairies and living in a fantasy world. You end up drifting aimlessly through life.

This is where your opposite sign of Virgo can help you, as all opposites of the zodiac complement each other. Virgo is the list-maker, the master of routine and an expert at order and organisation. Virgo's skill is in paying attention to the details of life and making a plan, so you know where you're heading and why. Virgo is also an earth sign, a reminder that you need to earth and ground yourself if you've become lost in Pisces' vast sea of emotion.

Your shadow side can also impact on your relationships with other people if you lose touch with reality or don't always tell the truth. You can end up being vague, and you would much prefer to tell a white lie than hurt someone else's feelings.

You can spin a good yarn too, and get carried away if the boundaries between truth and untruth become blurred. You lose sight of what's fake and what's real and will try to convince yourself and others that anything is true. Pisces' shadow side is lies and deceit, and your slippery nature means you get away with it, for a while at least.

Your Star Sign Secrets

Shhh, don't tell anyone but your greatest fear is that your acting abilities will be found out. You make a brilliant, tragic hero or heroine and, when necessary, you can pull on the heartstrings with a 'poor me' tale. You slip easily into the victim role, relinquishing responsibility for your part in any problem. Instead, you blame life, genes, even your star sign when things go wrong.

You do this to seek sympathy, as you want other people to take care of you or clear up your mess. You are a natural at playing any role, and you know how to seduce others into doing your bidding if you choose. This is Pisces' star sign secret.

You have another secret too, which is that you're gullible and other people can say or do anything to you and get away with it. The truth is that because you're so open and trusting, you are quickly led astray. Your natural default is to see the best in others too, so you have to take care that you're not easily fooled. Use your instincts to sniff out whether someone's genuine or insincere.

Your Love Life

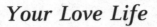

Knowing about your star sign is an absolute essential when it comes to love and relationships. Once you understand what drives you, nurtures you and keeps you happy in love, then you can be true to who you are rather than try to be someone you're not.

Plus, once you recognise your weak points when it comes to relationships (and everyone has them), you can learn to moderate them and focus instead on boosting your strengths to find happiness in love.

> **KEY CONCEPTS:** fairytale romance, tales of seduction and temptation, trusting wholeheartedly, your dream lover, learning to love yourself

Cosmic Tip: You are instinctively drawn towards people who need saving; if you want to be happy in love, be with someone who can look after and nurture you.

If you're a typical Pisces, you're an eternal romantic. Love for you is often way more than two people coming together to live happily side by side. Instead, the Pisces perspective on love can reach cosmic levels, as you look to find another person in life you can merge and become one with.

In fact, you are one of the star signs who's more likely to believe that the right person is out there, just waiting for you to discover them. Having this fantasy ideal partner in your head means it can be hard to find anyone who lives up to your idealistic expectations.

Similarly, you might project your fantasies onto another person, in a case of unrequited love. Your romantic sensibilities lead you to fall for people who are unavailable or don't feel the same way about you. When you don your rose-coloured glasses, you either can't see the truth of the situation or you don't want to accept what's real.

For the archetypal Pisces to be happy in love, it helps to throw the rose-coloured glasses away. Instead, seek out a partner who makes your heart leap, someone who's respectful of you and treats you the way you deserve.

Your giving, kind and understanding nature means that you make an excellent partner, and there are many happy Pisces love stories. You do have to learn to contain your love of fantasy within your relationship, however, and weave your spells of magic to keep the two of you close. If necessary, you might need to teach your partner to be romantic, and show them the joys of a loving and caring relationship.

Sometimes, your romantic inclination leads you on a merry dance, and your belief in true love means you fall in love time and again. Some of you are incurable romantics, who love the whole fairy-tale experience of love and marriage. The classic example is Elizabeth Taylor (27 February), who married eight times and twice to the same lover, Richard Burton. Their on-off love affair and union was one of the great love stories of recent times.

Your open-hearted and trusting nature means that you are predisposed towards love. In particular, you are often drawn towards poetic and soulful individuals: artists and musicians, creative and spiritual types. If someone seems vulnerable, you want to comfort them; if someone needs help, your caring nature responds; if someone bursts into tears, you feel their sorrow as if it were your own.

If you recognise these susceptibilities within yourself, it's vital that you learn to distinguish between real love and your Pisces tendency to define love as feeling needed. Invariably, this happens when you're looking for someone to complete you, or you believe that feeling needed will lead you to happiness.

If you're consistently disappointed by a string of lovers who let you down or don't appreciate you for who you are, take a step back and spend time by yourself. Self-love isn't a given birthright for you as a Pisces, because you're continually being pulled out of yourself to what lies beyond the ego.

When you truly love yourself for who you are, and are clear about the values you want and need to be happy in love, then you can start to seek out the relationship that's right for you.

It helps to be with someone who makes you laugh; and, most importantly, look for a partner who knows how to look after you and to nurture and care for you as much as you will for them. Seek out the partner who's happy to work hard for you, and your family if you choose to have one.

You don't need to lose your romantic nature to have a fulfilling relationship either; in fact, it's a bonus to any loving union. What you do need, however, is to respect and love yourself enough, so that you attract the right kind of person into your life.

Love can lose its rosy glow for you when the honeymoon period is over and romance dies. Then you need to find a way to deal with the practicalities of a relationship, to keep love alive. Your ideal partner will hold you firm and keep you grounded, and be happy to share responsibilities with you. If they allow you to escape now and again and encourage you to pursue your creative, spiritual or personal goals, so much the better.

Sometimes you say what you think your partner wants to hear, rather than being truthful, and learning to speak the truth within a relationship can take time. You are also prone to temptation, as your modern planet, Neptune, rules scandal and seduction.

Some Pisces individuals end up taking the lead role in their own romantic story or movie moment, creating their fantasy world in real life. You might choose to follow your heart wherever it leads, and throw caution to the winds and to heck with the consequences.

You never give up on the hope of finding true love and happiness in your life, however, even if it gets you into escapades and leads you down intriguing detours. At least you know you'll have some fantastic stories to tell the grandchildren about your fascinating and memorable romantic encounters.

Your Love Matches

Some star signs are a better love match for you than others. The classic combinations are the other two star signs from the same element as your sign, water; in Pisces' case, Cancer and Scorpio.

You are the zodiac's great romantic and the other water signs will match you when it comes to depth of feeling and emotion. Sometimes, however, you need a partner who acts as an anchor in your life and can ground you and keep love real. Usually, you work your way through a few lovers or partners before you find the one who's right for you.

It's also important to recognise that any star sign match can be a good match if you're willing to learn from each other and use astrological insight to understand more about what makes the other person tick. Here's a quick guide to your love matches with all twelve star signs:

Pisces–Aries: Next-Door Neighbours

An impulsive combination, the Pisces–Aries couple falls head over heels in love, and fast. Your emotional nature may wear thin on hard-nosed Aries, and Aries' impatience can drive you mad. If you meet each other halfway, your shared love and joy of life can be inspirational.

Pisces–Taurus: Sexy Sextiles

A romantic and profoundly sensual partnership, this combination brings out the best in you both.

The key to this relationship is whether you can ebb and flow together like the gentle lapping of the waves on a beach. Then you allow each other's creative and artistic natures to flourish and grow.

Pisces–Gemini: Squaring Up To Each Other

You two can be a crazy duo who love finding things out, exploring new ideas and venturing into new realms together. At its best, you are romantic buddies who walk hand in hand through life. A cosmic coupling that combines dreams and imagination with a quick and curious mind.

Pisces–Cancer: In Your Element

You two are super-sweet and want to take care of each other. There's a gentle vulnerability about this combination, and kindness and caring play a big part in the relationship. You both possess a sensitive soul, which does mean the tears are turned on more than usual.

Pisces–Leo: Soulmates

Pisces and Leo is a creative combination. Leo's love of drama and Pisces's colourful imagination conjures up a magical world. Both compassionate and caring types, you enjoy the pleasure to be gained from generous and giving acts of kindness.

Pisces–Virgo: Opposites Attract

You are the poet, the mystic, a soft touch. Virgo's the list-maker, the perfectionist who thrives on routine and an orderly universe. Together you teach each other about compassion and serving humanity. Finding a shared poetic muse becomes your inspiration for creativity and magic.

Pisces–Libra: Soulmates

Your sign of Pisces and the sign of Libra are ruled by Neptune and Venus respectively. Neptune is said to be the higher octave of Venus, and this is a musical, artistic and sensitive combination. An intuitive and romantic match that brings out the best in both of you.

Pisces–Scorpio: In Your Element

You two both want to feel deeply, and when you combine passion and intensity (Scorpio) with romance and bliss (Pisces), you have a relationship of epic proportions. A massive wave of love washes back and forth between you. You share a capacity to feel the whole gamut of emotions.

Pisces–Sagittarius: Squaring Up To Each Other

Ready to go on an adventure? You and Sagittarius are both ruled by big planet Jupiter. You two encourage each other to try out new things and experience life to the max. With a mutual understanding, you inspire and enrich each other's lives.

Pisces–Capricorn: Sexy Sextiles

Capricorn can be a workaholic but has a quiet and caring nature that you feel instinctively. If anyone is going to root out Capricorn's soft spot, it's you, mysterious, intuitive Pisces. You may be Capricorn's muse, but Capricorn provides the steady groundedness that you sometimes lack.

Pisces–Aquarius: Next-Door Neighbours

You and Aquarius are both hippies at heart, and an unconventional love affair appeals to you both. However, Aquarius can be too emotionally detached for your sensitive nature. If you learn to love each other's differences, then you can go the full distance in love.

Pisces–Pisces: Two Peas In A Pod

Romance is your domain, and this combination creates a warm and dreamy match. Fantasy enhances your lovemaking, and music, poetry and spirituality deepen your romantic perspective. As long as you stay grounded and keep in touch with reality, your love is heaven-sent.

Your Sex Life

• • • • •

As long as you're not harbouring any guilt or have been programmed to believe that sex is shameful, you are usually entirely at one with the idea of sexual abandonment and enjoying physical pleasure to the full.

You do have a tendency, however, to confuse sex with love as both arouse strong emotions within you. Mostly, you have a longing for intimacy with another human being, and sex often plays a significant role in your love of fantasy and romance.

There is a side to your Pisces nature that's incredibly seductive and alluring, and your mysterious, dreamy character acts like a magnet to people. There's a nod here to the theme of the siren in mythology or the mermaid in literature, both female Pisces archetypes. They both lured men into the deep sea, whether through their enchanting music or their beautiful voices.

If you're a classic Pisces, you understand the power of magic or, at least, recognise the potential of mystique and allure when it comes to attracting a lover. You seem to know instinctively what's sexy, and what to do to have someone desire you.

Two of the most iconic 'sex symbol' figures from the James Bond movies are played by Pisces actors. Fittingly for your star sign, which rules the sea, they both emerge from the water. The first was Ursula Andress (19 March), who played Bond Girl Honey Ryder in *Dr. No*, back in 1962. She rose out of the sea in her white bikini, complete with dagger and seashells, creating a classic James Bond moment.

The second was Daniel Craig (2 March) as James Bond himself, in *Casino Royale* in 2006. The scene of him walking out of the sea in tight blue trunks boosted him immediately to sex symbol status. It helps that both characters were dripping wet; if you haven't yet made love in the sea or water, this is a top Pisces fantasy.

Your vivid imagination means that wild fantasies and desires can enhance your love life. In fact, it's worth indulging this side of your character if you want to have great sex. Thinking about what you want to do when you meet a lover, getting yourself in the mood by reading erotic literature or watching blue movies or talking with your lover about each other's fantasies; all of these can add extra pleasure to the whole concept of sex and lovemaking.

It's not just about the time you spend together physically with a lover that turns you on, but what you conjure up in your head beforehand, and how you use the power of memory to recall thrilling moments. If you're a typical Pisces, it's the whole experience that brings something unique to the pleasures of sex.

Sex isn't only a physical pleasure for you either, and more than any other star sign, you are often aware of the spiritual nature of sexual intimacy. In fact, you might enjoy tantric sex, and learn how to hold back on orgasm to awaken kundalini sexual energy. Allow your fantasies and your desire for oneness to elevate the art of lovemaking to epic proportions.

PISCES ON A FIRST DATE

- you choose a romantic setting

- you turn up late because you got lost

- you wander around a museum or art gallery together

- you want to be entertained and feel inspired

- you know it's successful when you love their sense of humour

Your Friends and Family

As with many areas of your life, friendship can be a complicated process. More than any other star sign, you go with the flow. You can quite happily swim towards your friends but then go round in circles, lose your way and swim in the opposite direction.

In other words, you may have friends in your life who you don't see on a regular basis, but you still love to bits. Some of these friends might consider your level or style of friendship to be flaky, but what they need to understand is that you are loyal; just not in the way they expect.

You're not always the most reliable friend either, and your timekeeping skills can be questionable. That doesn't change the way you feel about your friends, however, and in your eyes, your behaviour doesn't indicate disrespect or not caring.

Alternatively, you team up with one group of friends in your life, only to change your mind at some point or find a new group of friends who you prefer being with. The Pisces nature is fluid, and sometimes there's no rhyme or reason to why you do what you do. Instead, you go where your emotions lead, and if you're in the mood for friendship and fun, great; if not and you want to be on your own, that's fine too, as far as you're concerned.

When you're on form, you are a delight to be around, and you can be exceptionally entertaining. You might be the Pisces individual with a crazy sense of humour who's always making your friends laugh, or the Pisces lover of stories, capable of weaving magical tales into the conversation.

You know how to have a good time, and if you're in the party mood, you'll be the one encouraging your friends to have one more drink or hit the dance floor. If you're feeling timid, however, you're more likely to be the friend propping up the bar.

You come alive when you're with people you enjoy being with, and especially those friends who teach you more about life, or always have something interesting to share with you. In fact, you come into your own when you find the people in life who share your particular interests or whose views on life mirror your own.

Also, you're attentive when friends are upset or sad, as this is when your caring nature kicks in.

You empathise strongly, and you'll be there with an encouraging speech as you mop up their tears. You'll be the first to defend your friend too, and remind them of their strengths and general loveliness.

When it comes to friendship, you have a unique sensitivity. This enables you to read between the lines, as if you hearing a pause in a piece of music. You pick up on subtle nuances and often know instinctively what your friends are thinking or feeling, or when to be in touch. Trust your psychic abilities, and learn to develop your sixth sense.

If a friendship becomes tedious or painful, you might turn tail and disappear. Your default setting is to swim away from trouble, and it's a similar story if you're around friends or colleagues who are toxic or negative. You pick up on bad vibes, and this can harm your sensitive nature.

Mingle with people in your life who are positive more of the time, and have a firm hold on the feel-good factor. Similarly, spend your time with friends who are real and sincere, and have their feet on the ground. This is especially important for you as it helps to ground you.

When it comes to your own family, here too you can ebb and flow, sometimes being evasive and other times connecting on a deep level. You're always present if there's a crisis to handle, but you often need your space away from your loved ones. This is especially important if they tend to remind you of all the weird things you used to do as a child, rather than love you unconditionally.

If you choose to become a parent, your kids often see you as a cross between crazy and creative, which ends up meaning you're lots of fun. You're not always the most organised parent, and discipline can go out the window.

Regular mealtimes and a tidy home aren't usually your top priorities when it comes to parenting. Where you do excel, however, is feeding your children's imaginations and encouraging them to read, to learn, to appreciate music and art, to be sensitive and caring and to explore life to the full.

Your children will quickly learn that it's okay to show your emotions and to say sorry if necessary. You do sometimes have to remember, however, that you're the parent and they're the child, and a full-blown meltdown in front of them is best avoided if possible.

Your Health and Well-Being

KEY CONCEPTS: water baby or nature lover, vegetarian or pescatarian, treat your body as a temple, live joyfully, raise your vibration

You are not traditionally the sportiest of all the star signs, and the physical body is rarely your priority. You tend to veer away from anything that smacks of routine or might cause you pain or distress. You can quickly talk yourself out of exercise, or even forget to turn up for a class.

The best exercise for you, therefore, is any activity that's fun or relaxing. Stretch your body if you can't be bothered to go to the gym or work out, or include dancing in your weekly schedule, whether you love the disco or you're into trance music.

If you're a water baby, indulge your fishy nature and swim as often as you like. This can be the perfect exercise when you live close to water or a swimming pool. An early morning dip can be meditative as well as being both relaxing and energising for your body.

Walking too is often a favourite activity for you, especially when you're in the beauty of nature. This has a restorative effect on you, and it's vital that you get away from it all on a boat or in the hills from time to time, especially if you live in a busy town or city.

For the typical Pisces, good health is a holistic concept, which incorporates mind, body and soul. If you know you're sensitive to external influences and you work in a caring role, or you're an empath or healer, it's imperative you pay attention to your well-being.

In this case, you'll be highly tuned in to vibration, and be aware of the boundless nature of your sign. If you hit psychic overwhelm, you need to retreat, wind down and recharge your batteries. You might choose to cleanse your aura or balance your chakras if you're a new age devotee.

In fact, all Pisces individuals benefit from time alone, quiet and solitude and plenty of sleep. Also, it's a good idea to have regular periods away from technology, gadgets and the digital world. You are one of the zodiac's givers, and if you over-give, you have nothing left to give yourself. Build quiet time and space in your life.

A trip to a spa can be restorative for you or create a sacred space at home, where you meditate or practise a ritual that's calming to you. This might be a comfy chair where you sit to relax, or an altar in your home, with individual objects or talismans that have personal significance for you and bring you a feeling of peace or security. This can be reassuring and a healthy way to replenish your energy.

Pisces rules the feet, and this is significant for you because your feet are how you connect to the earth. As a Pisces you can feel ungrounded or disconnected, so pay particular attention to your feet. Stand firm on the ground, and walk barefoot to feel the earth beneath your feet as often as you can. Reflexology works well for you too, or enjoying regular pedicures or foot massages.

Also, take care of your emotions and mood, as this can make a big difference to your well-being. Allow yourself time and space to daydream, to visualise where you're heading and why and to fantasise and cultivate happy thoughts. Learn what activities lift your mood and do more of them. The classic ones for your sign of Pisces are music, art, poetry, film and laughter.

Listen to your feelings on a regular basis and learn to know what you need in life to feel peaceful, nourished, blissed out or joyful.

Pisces and Food

Your traditional planet is Jupiter, linked to hedonism and indulgence, and it's often true for you as a Pisces that, when it comes to food and drink, you sometimes forget where the 'off' button is. Add to this the fact that you have an addictive nature, and your love of food or wine can become extreme.

Also, you are one of life's comfort eaters, and if you're feeling sad, you can quickly turn to the bottle or overindulge on biscuits. You do have to pay attention to your diet if you want to remain in good health, and not delude yourself that you're eating well or drinking moderately if you're not.

It is common for you to be vegetarian because you're an animal lover, although you often make an exception for fish, and follow a pescatarian diet. The classic Pisces enjoys all creatures of the sea, including scallops, sea urchins, clams and lobsters. You tend to like rich and creamy sauces with your seafood.

If you're on a health kick, it's a good idea to veer towards a fish or sea-related diet and try seaweed, sea vegetables or sushi. You might enjoy taking supplements that give the nod to your sign, such as blue-green algae or fish oil, or find juicing or healthy soups and shakes beneficial.

You need to take care what you put in your body as you can be sensitive to certain foods, drink or medicine. Your modern planet Neptune rules drugs and all liquids, including poisonous ones, so treat your body as a temple and don't feed it with harmful or toxic substances.

When it comes to making your food, you are frequently an inspired cook, and you love using your imagination and artistic flair to create recipes and put meals together. For a unique dinner party, you might like to develop a theme that links the food, decoration, even the dress code.

Eating out is often a Pisces pleasure, especially somewhere that has a romantic ambience with candlelight, soft music and divine cuisine. For a special occasion, choose a restaurant with a sea view.

Learn to be mindful of what you eat and drink but know that a strict diet rarely works for you. Instead, allow yourself indulgences, then rein yourself back in. Lead a joyful life, and feed your body well.

Do You Look Like A Pisces?

There's an ethereal quality to the classic Pisces, and you float along, sometimes looking as if you don't know where you're going or why. Your movements tend to be fluid.

You are usually on the short to average side, rather than particularly tall, although there are exceptions. Your body is often soft and fleshy, and you may have broad hips or be on the rounder side.

If you forget to eat, which is possible, some of you can look tiny, as if you need a big hug.

The face shape associated with Pisces is round, and you usually have pale skin and delicate features. The eyes are incredibly distinctive, whether you have a wide-eyed look or they're a baby blue colour. The eyes often look like pools you can dive into, and more than any other star sign, you show your emotions in your face.

Your hair is often fine, soft and silky, or out of control. The wild, natural look suits your artistic, poetic nature.

Your Style and Image

If one thing is true about Pisces' style, it's undefin-able. The fact is you take inspiration from any number of styles, and you often choose what to wear depending on your mood. You have such a vivid imagination that anything goes when it comes to clothes and it's not just the items of clothing, but the complete look that epitomises your style.

Take the late fashion designer Alexander McQueen (17 March), who was a brilliant exponent of theatrical fashion. His designs were romantic and bizarre with a sense of fantasy. He used body paint, clownish make-up, outrageously high shoes and outlandish headgear to create a unique look.

As a typical Pisces, you might choose a fashion style from a particular era in history and, depending on the way you express yourself through your clothes, this can change the way you feel.

Floaty and sensual clothes are your go-to items, anything that suggests romance, fluidity and flow. You look good in linen and soft fabrics that move with you. You take the indoors outdoors by wearing pyjama-style clothes or comfy yoga pants outside. Cashmere throws and fluffy scarves are popular too.

Classic Pisces colours represent the sea, and you look good in sea-green, aquamarine, silvers and whites. You can pull off any fashion, which means you often set trends too. Fashion designer Gloria Vanderbilt (20 February) was an early developer of designer blue jeans and one of the foremost names in jeans was Levi Strauss (26 February). Blue is of course a Pisces colour.

Your modern planet, Neptune, is associated with glamour, and a typical Pisces loves getting dressed up for a big night out. Sparkle and shimmer, sequins and glitz and flowing hair conjure up a romantic mood. Fancy dress parties are a Pisces' dream.

You can be equally happy, however, wearing your oldest cardigan, a faded T-shirt and much-loved jeans with holes in. Pisces men wear the struggling artist look well, sometimes with long hair and beard to match.

Never forget your Pisces love of shoes. Your sign rules the feet and whether you idolise dainty pumps and pretty sandals, or you fancy wearing

Alexander McQueen's 30-cm Armadillo shoes shaped like a lobster's claw, always pay attention to your feet and footwear.

Your Home

Your Ideal Pisces Home:

A luxury coastal home on a hill with a private beach, away from prying eyes. Surrounded by windows on three sides, so you have a sea view from every room. The sound of the sea lulls you to sleep at night.

You are one of the water signs and your modern planet Neptune governs the sea. Living close to water has a therapeutic effect on you, and many Pisces individuals gravitate towards homes close to rivers or lakes, on boats or islands.

As a Pisces, it's essential if you don't live near the sea or another body of water to have plenty of water around your home. This can take the form of glass vases filled with flowers, bowls of water with coloured stones, an aquarium or a fountain or rock pool in the garden.

The bathroom is often your favourite room in the house, so ensure you decorate it in a way that fits your romantic soul. This can include a seaside theme with a wave effect on the walls and motifs of fishes, shells and anchors. Pride of place will be a large bath you can luxuriate in, surrounded by candles.

The colours associated with Pisces are blues, sea-green, aquamarine and mauve. White is also a good colour choice for your home, with its theme of purity, or go for translucent colours and silvery tones that change with the light.

Sometimes you like to change around your furnishings to suit your mood. You might have two sets of curtains, one for summer and one for winter, or alternative covers for a comfy chair. Subdued lighting creates atmosphere and carefully positioned lamps and candles can change your surroundings, depending on the time of day and night.

Your style is often theatrical with a grand bed taking centre stage in the bedroom, for example, or decorative features from different eras and cultures. You appreciate rich, sensuous materials, such as velvets and silks, and floaty fabrics, such as light muslin or linen. Soft and curvy lines are easier on the eye than hard corners, and you prefer subtlety rather than sharp, definite patterns or colours.

There must be plenty for you to look at, for your inner artist to enjoy and savour. Beautiful objects, pictures of landscapes or seascapes, a mural painted on the wall. You're a lover of music too, whether you have a piano, or CDs or vinyl providing a wide choice of musical genres.

If you're a typical Pisces, you have a sentimental nature, and photos of loved ones, family and friends take pride of place, ideally in silver and antique photo frames.

Most importantly, however, your home will be a place where old and new friends can come to relax and share a glass of wine, and where even the most personal emotions can be expressed.

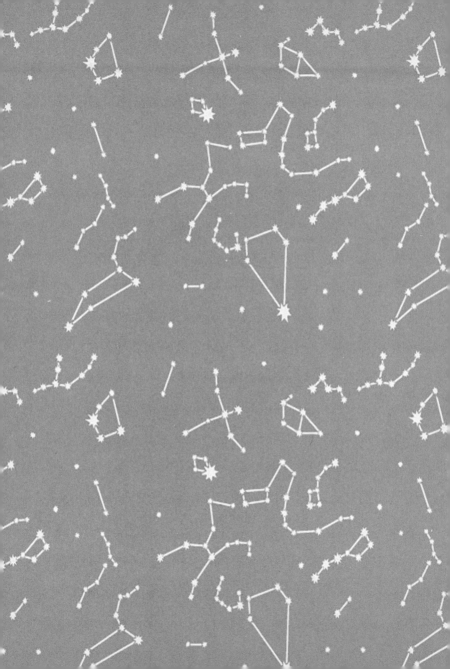

Your Star Sign Destinations

IDEAS FOR PISCES:

• *a week scuba diving in the Red Sea*

• *an eco-friendly beach holiday*

• *visit an elephant sanctuary in Indonesia*

Did you know that many cities and countries are ruled by a particular star sign? This is based on when a country was founded, although, depending on their history, sometimes places have more than one star sign attributed to them.

This can help you decide where to go on holiday, and it can also be why there are certain places where you feel at home straight away.

As a Pisces, you often find it hard deciding where to go on holiday. If this is you, it's a good idea to organise a few short trips if you can't make up your mind, rather than go all in on a big trip away. Your changeable nature enjoys being in different surroundings.

The sea is an undeniable pull for you because it's somewhere you can dream and let your imagination roam. Also, anywhere with beautiful scenery is a plus, as this unlocks your artistic nature.

You might choose to go and live on a boat, on a sailing holiday or a barge trip on canals. Ideally, you prefer to be away from large crowds and too much noise. Peace and tranquillity are signature features for the ideal Pisces break. You need time away from all the busy-ness to tap into your inner soul and spirit.

You don't usually like temperatures that are too hot or too cold – nothing too extreme – but going somewhere you can switch off completely does appeal to you. You like going somewhere you can relax, try the local tipple and be indulgent, but you often prefer a deeper, more mystical experience.

Countries ruled by Pisces include Portugal, North Africa, Mauritius

Cities Bournemouth and Grimsby in the UK; Cowes on the Isle of Wight; Seville and Santiago de Compostela in Spain; Christchurch in New Zealand; Jerusalem; Warsaw in Poland; Alexandria in Egypt

Your Career and Vocation

KEY CONCEPTS: fertile and creative imagination, caring professions, follow your dream, lead from your heart, inspired ideas

As a Pisces, you are one of the most versatile and adaptable of all the star signs and, when it comes to your career, it's important not to limit your options. The more you are in touch with your dreams and able to bring them to life and make them real, the more successful you're likely to be. Think vocation rather than job or profession, and you're on the right track.

What tends to be of utmost importance for you when it comes to your career is that you're invested emotionally in what you do. This is what will make the difference, and be most satisfying and fulfilling for you in the long run.

Many Pisces individuals are drawn towards careers where you can help and heal others, professions where an emotional connection is paramount. You have a natural sensitivity and ability to empathise, and you often develop a deep bond with your clients, your patients, the people you work with on a one-to-one basis.

Also, you are usually willing to sacrifice yourself to help others. Your immense compassion and kindness call you to save lost souls, to be there for people or animals who are weak or vulnerable. Some of you spend your whole life on a mission to heal the sick, to tend to the wounded, and you are a natural at counselling, listening and finding new ways to solve problems.

If you're a typical Pisces, you have a fertile and creative imagination, and this leads you to excel in many different professions. You are at your best when you can work with your ideas. If a boss wants to get the best out of you, they need to give you creative licence to follow where your imagination takes you.

All the water signs are said to be 'mute' because your initial response is through your feelings. Add to this the fact that your co-ruler Neptune rules images, and the visual world is where you're most at home. Photography, film-making, art and design; all the creative industries: this is where you find many Pisces individuals making their mark.

Acting too tends to be a popular choice, but for another reason. This is where you get to put on a character and step into a different role. This highlights the side of your Pisces nature that's chameleon-like. You are rarely rigid or fixed about anything; instead, you are continually shifting your attitude, changing your thoughts and influenced by your fluctuating moods.

This is why fantasy appeals to you, because it's fictional and you can make it up as you go along. In a fantasy world, you can be whoever you want to be. Take this into account, and it's not surprising that you rarely fit happily in a nine-to-five role or a work routine that's too inflexible or uniform.

If you do work in a regular job, then it's imperative that you have an interest outside of your work that allows you to indulge your love of fantasy and express your artistic nature.

The archetypal Pisces has no shortage of ideas or dreams you want to fulfil. The challenge comes for you, however, in choosing what to do, and focusing on it wholeheartedly. If you don't apply yourself or home in on one project at a time, you can lose focus. You're easily distracted, and without a specific target or a goal, you can drift along aimlessly.

Seek out what awakens you in life, and commit yourself to it. In other words, do what you love. As a Pisces, you are tuned in to the zeitgeist. Your vivid imagination can take you soaring into space, keen to further scientific knowledge, or take you deep down into the collective unconscious and retrieve what's been forgotten, so you can use it in your art to inspire others.

Time on your own can help to unlock your dreams, and being away from noise or negativity is wise too. You tend to be sensitive to criticism, and averse to competitive people. Instead, seek out collaborative ventures that feed your soul, and stay true to your romantic, yearning nature.

Be a dancer, like Nureyev (17 March) or Nijinsky (12 March), be a poet or fantasy writer, like

Elizabeth Barrett Browning (6 March) or Dr Seuss (2 March), but most importantly, be true to you.

If you're seeking inspiration for a new job, take a look at the list below, which reveals the traditional careers that come under the Pisces archetype:

TRADITIONAL PISCES CAREERS

marine biologist

deep sea diver

sailor

composer

poet/artist

brewer

oil industry employee

pharmaceutical worker

clairvoyant/psychic

art/music therapist

photographer

nurse

actor/film industry

chiropodist

mental health worker
priest
charity worker
animal rescue helper
swimming instructor
meditation teacher

Your Money and Prosperity

You have a complicated attitude towards money because, if you're a typical Pisces, you are not at all materialistic or bothered about possessions. You understand there's more to life than material goals, and life's riches are rarely to be found in luxury items or status symbols.

Also, there's an aspect to Pisces, in your role as last sign of the zodiac, that is about letting go and releasing what you have to find spiritual fulfilment. Also, Pisces' inherent values in life often lean towards social responsibility and sharing out equally the world's resources.

The archetypal Pisces also has a strong faith and belief that life will provide for you, and you're often trusting in your approach to money and prosperity. Some Pisces individuals take this one stage further and give up everything to follow a religious path or surrender entirely to wherever life leads.

This is all well and good but, at the same time, this perspective on life won't necessarily feed you or keep a roof over your head. Therefore, to live in the real world, it's helpful if you learn to balance your trusting, giving ways with a more practical approach towards money and finances.

If you already know that the words 'budgeting' and 'balancing the books' bring you out in a cold sweat, turn to other people for financial expertise and advice. At the very least, learn to open your bills as soon as they come through the letterbox, instead of turning into the metaphorical ostrich and burying your head in the sand.

The classic Pisces finds accounting annoying, but where you do excel when it comes to money and prosperity is using your Pisces credentials to be successful. Know your strengths, and put them to good use in the world. Take Steve Jobs (24 February), for example, co-founder of Apple Inc., who was a visionary and a creative genius. He utilised his unique skills, and in the process became a billionaire.

As a Pisces, you have a myriad of ideas that you can use to influence other people, to solve problems, to take what's already known or fixed in the world and deliver it in such a way that it comes across as new, innovative or inspirational.

For you, money and wealth is often a by-product of being successful.

Where you have to be careful when it comes to money is your trusting nature. You are vulnerable to sob stories, and you're a soft touch because you don't like to hear about other people's pain or troubles without wanting to help. If anyone's going to be seduced or scammed or be talked out of their money, it's you.

That's not to say you're going to fall for the next internet scam, but you do need to consider how far you take your natural instinct to help and care for others. If a friend or family member is in need, be there for them on an emotional level but think twice before you help out financially.

In fact, this is a wise approach for you in general when it comes to money. Be clear about why you're investing in someone or something. Use your natural instincts to avoid the lost causes, and steer yourself towards worthy causes and prosperous investments. Engage your brain, and not just your emotional response.

Your Cosmic Gifts and Talents

Romance

You put the romance into life with your kind-hearted nature and your willingness to open your heart to love time and again. Romance conjures up feelings of excitement and mystery. It filters out the harsh realities of life, as you view the world through your rose-coloured glasses. It's a soft tint on a harsh background; it's a waft of perfume that delights your nose; it's a bunch of beautifully coloured flowers. Be the zodiac's representative for romance and fill the world with love.

Stargazer

One of your roles as a Pisces is to search for the cord between the individual and the universe, the connection between the microcosm and the macrocosm. You go beyond yourself as far as the eye can see, and further still to reach infinite dimensions. You are the stargazer and cosmonaut of the zodiac.

Nicolaus Copernicus (19 February) placed the Sun at the centre of the universe, astronomer Patrick Moore (4 March) was enthusiastic about his love for the cosmos and physicist Brian Cox (3 March) continues the legacy of Pisces' fascination with the stars. Stargazing is a reminder that you are a tiny speck in the grandeur of the universe. Be a stargazer to discover the true definition of awe and wonder.

Empathy

You cannot help but give to other people, and your natural instincts for caring and compassion are selfless. You empathise with people's emotions; you teach other people through your own experiences in life, whether good or bad or in-between. You connect with other people on a deep level because you feel what they feel. This gives you a unique ability to bond with others, to make connections that transcend race, culture or gender and, ultimately, to play a significant role in healing the suffering in the world. Your empathy is a powerful tool.

Creative Designer

You are the ideas merchant of the zodiac, and your creativity knows no bounds. You sail forth on the wings of inspiration, seeking expression for your artistic and creative soul. Whether there's an artist in you, a poet, a dancer, a music-maker, tap into your Pisces inheritance and your rich creative source. Your Pisces creativity can ensoul the world.

Mad Professor

You have a special place in the zodiac because you are the culmination of all twelve signs. This means that, theoretically, all the knowledge and wisdom of the world is inherent within you. Therefore, be passionately curious and go wherever your fascination and desire for learning takes you.

The term 'passionately curious' is attributed to one of life's most brilliant mad professors, Albert Einstein (14 March), who was a Pisces genius. Was he a genius because he had a brilliant brain that disposed him to be a physicist, or did his love for physics and music cause his brain to grow and expand? There's not a definitive answer, but it's your Pisces birthright to learn and explore to the full.

Go With The Flow

You are not put off by anything rigid or fixed in life. In fact, you believe that everything in life is potentially changeable, and you will look for the opening, the nuance, the inlet that gains you entrance. Your ability to go with the flow and be malleable and adaptable takes you to places other people don't even think about. Water seeps into cracks and finds a way through the invisible pores of stone. As a Pisces, you explore all options and then some. Go with the flow, and consider everything from a new and fresh angle.

Cosmic Humour

You look at life uniquely, because you see things from an unusual perspective, and this shows in your comedic approach. Many Pisces individuals are naturally funny, like popular comedian Michael McIntyre (21 February).

You are known for your satire too, and one of the most ingenious and hilariously funny and surreal works in this area of recent times is *The Hitchhiker's Guide to the Galaxy* by Douglas Adams (11 March). Starting as a radio comedy in 1978, it was then developed into books, which quickly took on cult status. The books have a cosmic theme, and the title of the fourth one in the series is fitting for a Pisces: *So Long, And Thanks for All The Fish*.

Films, Books, Music

• • • • •

Films: *The Big Blue*, director Luc Besson (18 March) or *The Sixth Sense* starring Pisces Bruce Willis (19 March)

Books: *Les Misérables* by Victor Hugo (26 February) or *Gone Girl* by Gillian Flynn (24 February) or *On The Road* by Jack Kerouac (12 March)

Music: Music is in Pisces' DNA, and you can choose from a complete range of classical composers, modern singers and songwriters. Here are a few: Delibes (21 February), Vera Lynn (20 March), Harry Belafonte (1 March), George Harrison (25 February), Johnny Cash (26 February), Al Jarreau (12 March), Will.i.am (15 March), Rihanna (15 March)

YOGA POSE:

Toe Squat: opens toes and feet,
strengthens ankles

TAROT CARD:

The High Priestess

GIFTS TO BUY A PISCES:

- a book of love poems
- a pedicure voucher
- 'name a star' gift set
- a musical instrument
- sailing lessons
- mermaid blanket
- Diptyque candles
- silk pyjamas
- a steam room
- Star Gift – a vineyard

Pisces Celebrities Born On Your Birthday

FEBRUARY

 19 Copernicus, Benicio del Toro, Prince Andrew, Beth Ditto, Victoria Justice, Millie Bobby Brown, Seal

 20 Sidney Poitier, Mike Leigh, Robert Altman, Nancy Wilson, Brenda Blethyn, Gloria Vanderbilt, Ivana Trump, Cindy Crawford, Kurt Cobain, Jay Hernandez, Rihanna

21 Delibes, Hubert de Givenchy, Anaïs Nin, Jilly Cooper, Nina Simone, Rue McClanahan, Alan Rickman, Kelsey Grammer, Jack Coleman, William Baldwin, Jennifer Love Hewitt, Imogen Stubbs, Charlotte Church, Corbin Bleu, Ellen Page, Ashley Greene

22 George Washington, Bruce Forsyth, Sheila Hancock, Julie Walters, Kenneth Williams, Kyle MacLachlan, Steve Irwin, Jeri Ryan, Chris Moyles, Drew Barrymore, James Blunt

23 Peter Fonda, Kristin Davis, Tamsin Greig, Dakota Fanning, Emily Blunt

24 Emmanuelle Riva, Steve Jobs, Edward James Olmos, Dennis Waterman, Billy Zane, Floyd Mayweather

25 Renoir, George Harrison, Lee Evans, Téa Leoni, Ed Balls, Chelsea Handler

26 Victor Hugo, Fats Domino, Johnny Cash, Michael Bolton, Erykah Badu

 27 Joanne Woodward, Elizabeth Taylor, Timothy Spall, Peter Andre, Chelsea Clinton, Josh Groban

 28 Brian Jones, Stephanie Beacham, Ainsley Harriott, Ali Larter, Natalia Vodianova, Noureen DeWulf, Olivia Palermo

 29 Tony Robbins, Ja Rule

MARCH

 1 David Niven, Harry Belafonte, Glenn Miller, Catherine Bach, Roger Daltrey, Ron Howard, Tim Daly, Jensen Ackles, Justin Bieber, Javier Bardem, Paul Hollywood, Kesha, Lupita Nyong'o

 2 Dr Seuss, Lou Reed, Karen Carpenter, Jon Bon Jovi, Daniel Craig, John Altman,

Rebel Wilson, Chloe Green, Chris Martin, Becky G.

 3 Jean Harlow, Miranda Richardson, Ronan Keating, Alex Zane, Brian Cox, Jessica Biel, Charlie Brooker, Camila Cabello

 4 Patrick Moore, Sam Taylor-Johnson, Patsy Kensit, Brooklyn Beckham, Len Wiseman

5 Michelangelo, Rex Harrison, Elaine Paige, Andy Gibb, Shaquille O'Neal, Matt Lucas, Eva Mendes, Madison Beer, Niki Taylor

 6 Frankie Howerd, Kiri Te Kanawa, David Gilmour, Tom Arnold, Alan Davies, Betty Boo

7 Rachel Weisz, Matthew Vaughn, Rik Mayall, Laura Prepon, Bryan Cranston, E. L. James, Tom Chaplin

8 Cyd Charisse, Anselm Kiefer, Gary Numan, Aidan Quinn, Freddie Prinze Jr

 9 Raúl Juliá, Bobby Fischer, Juliette Binoche, Isabella Hervey, Bow Wow, Oscar Isaac, Brittany Snow, Barbie

 10 Chuck Norris, Sharon Stone, Eva Herzigova, Jon Hamm, Carrie Underwood, Rafe Spall, Shannon Tweed, Olivia Wilde, Robin Thicke, Neneh Cherry

 11 Rupert Murdoch, Douglas Adams, Shane Richie, Laurence Llewelyn-Bowen, Johnny Knoxville, Alex Kingston, Joel Madden, Benji Madden, Thora Birch, Terrence Howard

 12 Nijinsky, Anish Kapoor, Jack Kerouac, Liza Minnelli, James Taylor, Al Jarreau, Aaron Eckhart, Christina Grimmie, Pete Doherty, Elly Jackson

13 L Ron Hubbard, Neil Sedaka, William H. Macy, Linda Robson, Emile Hirsch, Dana Delany

14 Albert Einstein, Diane Arbus, Michael Caine, Quincy Jones, Jasper Carrott, Billy Crystal, Chris Klein, Ansel Elgort, Stephen Curry, Simone Biles, Jamie Bell

15 David Cronenberg, Judd Hirsch, Philip Green, Terence Trent D'Arby, Ry Cooder, Penny Lancaster, Eva Longoria, will.i.am

 16 Jerry Lewis, Isabella Huppert, Jimmy Nail, Peaches Geldof

17 Nat King Cole, Rudolf Nureyev, Patrick Duffy, Kurt Russell, Rob Lowe, Billy Corgan, Bruce Parry, Patti Hansen, Justin Hawkins, Stephen Gately, Coco Austin, Alexander McQueen, Rob Kardashian

Luc Besson, Vanessa Williams, Queen Latifah, Adam Levine, Marvin Humes, Lily Collins

 Tommy Cooper, Ursula Andress, Glenn Close, Bruce Willis, Julien Macdonald

 Vera Lynn, William Hurt, Spike Lee, Holly Hunter, Steve McFadden, Glennon Doyle Melton, Ruby Rose

Q&A Section

• • • • •

Q. What is the difference between a Sun sign and a Star sign?

A. They are the same thing. The Sun spends one month in each of the twelve star signs every year, so if you were born on 1 January, you are a Sun Capricorn. In astronomy, the Sun is termed a star rather than a planet, which is why the two names are interchangeable. The term 'zodiac sign', too, means the same as Sun sign and Star sign and is another way of describing which one of the twelve star signs you are, e.g. Sun Capricorn.

Q. What does it mean if I'm born on the cusp?

A. Being born on the cusp means that you were born on a day when the Sun moves from one of the twelve zodiac signs into the next. However, the Sun doesn't change signs at the same time each year. Sometimes it can be a day earlier or a day later. In the celebrity birthday section of the book, names in brackets mean that this person's birthday falls into this category.

If you know your complete birth data, including the date, time and place you were born, you can find out definitively what Sun sign you are. You do this by either checking an ephemeris (a planetary table) or asking an astrologer. For example, if a baby were born on 20 January 2018, it would be Sun Capricorn if born before 03:09 GMT or Sun Aquarius if born after 03:09 GMT. A year earlier, the Sun left Capricorn a day earlier and entered Aquarius on 19 January 2017, at 21:24 GMT. Each year the time changes are slightly different.

Q. Has my sign of the zodiac changed since I was born?

A. Every now and again, the media talks about a new sign of the zodiac called Ophiuchus and about there now being thirteen signs. This means that you're unlikely to be the same Sun sign as you always thought you were.

This method is based on fixing the Sun's movement to the star constellations in the sky, and is called 'sidereal' astrology. It's used traditionally in India and other Asian countries.

The star constellations are merely namesakes for the twelve zodiac signs. In western astrology, the zodiac is divided into twelve equal parts that are in sync with the seasons. This method is called 'tropical' astrology. The star constellations and the zodiac signs aren't the same.

Astrology is based on a beautiful pattern of symmetry (see Additional Information) and it wouldn't be the same if a thirteenth sign were introduced into the pattern. So never fear, no one is going to have to say their star sign is Ophiuchus, a name nobody even knows how to pronounce!

Q. Is astrology still relevant to me if I was born in the southern hemisphere?

A. Yes, astrology is unquestionably relevant to you. Astrology's origins, however, were founded in the northern hemisphere, which is why the Spring Equinox coincides with the Sun's move into Aries, the first sign of the zodiac. In the southern hemisphere, the seasons are reversed. Babylonian, Egyptian and Greek and Roman astrology are the forebears of modern-day astrology, and all of these civilisations were located in the northern hemisphere.

• • • • •

Q. Should I read my Sun sign, Moon sign and Ascendant sign?

A. If you know your horoscope or you have drawn up an astrology wheel for the time of your birth, you will be aware that you are more than your Sun sign. The Sun is the most important star in the sky, however, because the other planets revolve around it, and your horoscope in the media is based on Sun signs. The Sun represents your essence, who you are striving to become throughout your lifetime.

The Sun, Moon and Ascendant together give you a broader impression of yourself as all three reveal further elements about your personality. If you know your Moon and Ascendant signs, you can read all three books to gain further insight into who you are. It's also a good idea to read the Sun sign book that relates to your partner, parents, children, best friends, even your boss for a better understanding of their characters too.

Q. Is astrology a mix of fate and free will?

A. Yes. Astrology is not causal, i.e. the planets don't cause things to happen in your life; instead, the two are interconnected, hence the saying 'As above, so below'. The symbolism of the planets' movements mirrors what's happening on earth and in your personal experience of life.

You can choose to sit back and let your life unfold, or you can decide the best course of action available to you. In this way, you are combining your fate and free will, and this is one of astrology's major purposes in life. A knowledge of astrology can help you live more authentically, and it offers you a fresh perspective on how best to make progress in your life.

Q. What does it mean if I don't identify with my Sun sign? Is there a reason for this?

A. The majority of people identify with their Sun sign, and it is thought that one route to fulfilment is to grow into your Sun sign. You do get the odd exception, however.

For example, a Pisces man was adamant that he wasn't at all romantic, mystical, creative or caring, all typical Pisces archetypes. It turned out he'd spent the whole of his adult life working in the oil industry and lived primarily on the sea. Neptune is one of Pisces' ruling planets and god of the sea and Pisces rules all liquids, including oil. There's the Pisces connection.

Q. What's the difference between astrology and astronomy?

A. Astrology means 'language of the stars', whereas astronomy means 'mapping of the stars'. Traditionally, they were considered one discipline, one form of study and they coexisted together for many hundreds of years. Since the dawn of the Scientific Age, however, they have split apart.

Astronomy is the scientific strand, calculating and logging the movement of the planets, whereas astrology is the interpretation of the movement of the stars. Astrology works on a symbolic and intuitive level to offer guidance and insight. It reunites you with a universal truth, a knowingness that can sometimes get lost in place of an objective, scientific truth. Both are of value.

Q. What is a cosmic marriage in astrology?

A. One of the classic indicators of a relation-ship that's a match made in heaven is the union of the Sun and Moon. When they fall close to each other in the same sign in the birth charts of you and your partner, this is called a cosmic marriage. In astrology, the Sun and Moon are the king and queen of the heavens; the Sun is a masculine energy, and the Moon a feminine energy. They represent the eternal cycle of day and night, yin and yang.

Q. What does the Saturn Return mean?

A. In traditional astrology, Saturn was the furthest planet from the Sun, representing boundaries and the end of the universe. Saturn is linked to karma and time, and represents authority, structure and responsibility. It takes Saturn twenty-nine to thirty years to make a complete cycle of the zodiac and return to the place where it was when you were born.

This is what people mean when they talk about their Saturn Return; it's the astrological coming of age. Turning thirty can be a soul-searching time, when you examine how far you've come in life and whether you're on the right track. It's a watershed moment, a reality check and a defining stage of adulthood. The decisions you make during your Saturn Return are crucial, whether they represent endings or new commitments. Either way, it's the start of an important stage in your life path.

Additional Information

• • • • •

The Symmetry of Astrology

There is a beautiful symmetry to the zodiac (see horoscope wheel). There are twelve zodiac signs, which can be divided into two sets of 'introvert' and 'extrovert' signs, four elements (fire, earth, air, water), three modes (cardinal, fixed, mutable) and six pairs of opposite signs.

One of the values of astrology is in bringing opposites together, showing how they complement each other and work together and, in so doing, restore unity. The horoscope wheel represents the cyclical nature of life.

Aries (*March 21–April 19*)
Taurus (*April 20–May 20*)
Gemini (*May 21–June 20*)
Cancer (*June 21–July 22*)
Leo (*July 23–August 22*)
Virgo (*August 23–September 22*)
Libra (*September 23–October 23*)
Scorpio (*October 24–November 22*)
Sagittarius (*November 23–December 21*)
Capricorn (*December 22–January 20*)
Aquarius (*January 21–February 18*)
Pisces (*February 19–March 20*)

ELEMENTS

There are four elements in astrology and three signs allocated to each. The elements are:

fire – Aries, Leo, Sagittarius
earth – Taurus, Virgo, Capricorn
air – Gemini, Libra, Aquarius
water – Cancer, Scorpio, Pisces

What each element represents:

Fire – fire blazes bright and fire types are inspirational, motivational, adventurous and love creativity and play

Earth – earth is grounding and solid, and earth rules money, security, practicality, the physical body and slow living

Air – air is intangible and vast and air rules thinking, ideas, social interaction, debate and questioning

Water – water is deep and healing and water rules feelings, intuition, quietness, relating, giving and sharing

MODES

There are three modes in astrology and four star signs allocated to each. The modes are:

cardinal – Aries, Cancer, Libra, Capricorn
fixed – Taurus, Leo, Scorpio, Aquarius
mutable – Gemini, Virgo, Sagittarius, Pisces

What each mode represents:

Cardinal – The first group represents the leaders of the zodiac, and these signs love to initiate and take action. Some say they're controlling.

Fixed – The middle group holds fast and stands the middle ground and acts as a stable, reliable companion. Some say they're stubborn.

Mutable – The last group is more willing to go with the flow and let life drift. They're more flexible and adaptable and often dual-natured. Some say they're all over the place.

INTROVERT AND EXTROVERT SIGNS/ OPPOSITE SIGNS

The introvert signs are the earth and water signs and the extrovert signs are the fire and air signs. Both sets oppose each other across the zodiac.

The 'introvert' earth and water oppositions are:

- Taurus – • Scorpio
- Cancer – • Capricorn
- Virgo – • Pisces

The 'extrovert' air and fire oppositions are:

- Aries – • Libra
- Gemini – • Sagittarius
- Leo – • Aquarius

THE HOUSES

The houses of the astrology wheel are an additional component to Sun sign horoscopes. The symmetry that is inherent within astrology remains, as the wheel is divided into twelve equal sections, called 'houses'. Each of the twelve houses is governed by one of the twelve zodiac signs.

There is an overlap in meaning as you move round the houses. Once you know the symbolism of all the star signs, it can be fleshed out further by learning about the areas of life represented by the twelve houses.

The houses provide more specific information if you choose to have a detailed birth chart reading.

This is based not only on your day of birth, which reveals your star sign, but also your time and place of birth. Here's the complete list of the meanings of the twelve houses and the zodiac sign they are ruled by:

1 – **Aries:** self, physical body, personal goals

2 – **Taurus:** money, possessions, values

3 – **Gemini:** communication, education, siblings, local neighbourhood

4 – **Cancer:** home, family, roots, the past, ancestry

5 – **Leo:** creativity, romance, entertainment, children, luck

6 – **Virgo:** work, routine, health, service

7 – **Libra:** relationships, the 'other', enemies, contracts

8 – **Scorpio:** joint finances, other people's resources, all things hidden and taboo

9 – **Sagittarius:** travel, study, philosophy, legal affairs, publishing, religion

10 – **Capricorn:** career, vocation, status, reputation

11 – **Aquarius:** friends, groups, networks, social responsibilities

12 – **Pisces:** retreat, sacrifice, spirituality

A GUIDE TO LOVE MATCHES

The star signs relate to each other in different ways depending on their essential nature. It can also be helpful to know the pattern they create across the zodiac. Here's a quick guide that relates to the chapter on Love Matches:

Two Peas In A Pod – the same star sign

Opposites Attract – star signs opposite each other

Soulmates – five or seven signs apart, and a traditional 'soulmate' connection

In Your Element – four signs apart, which means you share the same element

Squaring Up To Each Other – three signs apart, which means you share the same mode

Sexy Sextiles – two signs apart, which means you're both 'introverts' or 'extroverts'

Next Door Neighbours – one sign apart, different in nature but often share close connections